HERMOSILLO
MEXICO

ENTRANCE TO RAMON CORRAL PARK

Notes Regarding This Tome

In re-issuing this book, I have endeavored to provide the reader with a faithful reproduction of the original. The covers are the original covers and the text and illustrations within are also the originals, though the photographs have been slightly enhanced with contrast.

During my research about this book and its author, I encountered a few other pieces that will be of interest and have included them in the end of the original. These include a letter from the President of Sonora to the Sunset Homeseekers' Bureau (the original publisher), an advertisement for land in Hermosillo from *Sunset*, and what I believe is the first published short story from Bourdon Wilson, the author.

The exact year of publication of this volume is not readily available but within the text, there is reference to a set of statistics from 1900-1909. Further, given Wilson's January 1911 article in *Sunset* about Hermosillo and the ad of land for sale in Hermosillo in the same volume offering an "illustrated booklet" – presumably a copy of this same one you are holding now – I shall put the initial publication date at 1910.

About the Author

Bourdon Wilson began his writing career as a short story author. My research shows his first published piece was part of *Frank Leslie's Popular Monthly* in 1899, titled "A Mexican Conjugation of the Verb 'To Love'". That short story is included as a bonus section at the end of this very book. By 1906, more short stories by Wilson had been published in *The Argonaut*, *Sunset* magazine, and in smaller newspapers and publications. One such story, "The Donkey and the Gringo: An Adventure in Chihuahua," has tones of an autobiographical nature and he references working for the Rio Verde Mining Company in Chihuahua, Mexico, which is the state located next to Sonora, where Hermosillo is located. Whether Wilson was employed by the Rio Verde Mining Company (or if any such company even existed) remains unclear. However, it does seem evident to me that Wilson lived in and around Mexico at various points over the years and was even quoted in 1905 about the orange production in Hermosillo.

Over the years, Bourdon Wilson authored several articles and other tomes extolling the beauty and benefits of various locales around California for the Sunset Homeseekers' Bureau and *Sunset*. A number of these "illustrated booklets" from areas in California will be reprinted and available in the coming months from The Press of Ill Repute.

Additionally, Wilson co-authored one full-length book with Arthur Howard Noll in 1911. *In Quest of Aztec Treasure* is a fictionalized travel adventure around Mexico and will be another forthcoming title in the ¡Viva Mexico! series from The Press of Ill Repute.

About the Original Publisher

The Sunset Homeseekers' Bureau was an arm of *Sunset* magazine, which was originally conceived by Southern Pacific Railroad. In the late 1800s, railroad companies were seeking to increase ridership and take advantage of the influx of the California curious. Southern Pacific undertook an ambitious program of producing lavishly illustrated print brochures about stops on their routes and distributing them through their network of stations and train lines. In 1898, they added *Sunset*, a magazine about sights and adventures along their lines.

Less than two years later, they had a circulation of 15,000 nationwide, including libraries, newspapers, schools, and individuals. By 1904, the page count jumped from 32 pages to a hefty 208 with a readership of more than 50,000. By 1911, Sunset was read by more than 500,000 people each month. During this period, Southern Pacific Railroad added a "Development Section" to Sunset. This Development Section supplemental section inside *Sunset* (created by the new Sunset Homeseekers' Bureau) often featured smaller cities and articles on the benefits of said cities. Sunset used its writers and publishing facilities to create hundreds of promotional brochures and pamphlets on these smaller towns, in effect, acting as a Chamber of Commerce. Initially, the focus was on California but they expanded throughout the Southwest and, in the case of this piece, all the way into Mexico.

Today, *Sunset* is still in publication, though Southern Pacific Railroad is no longer the owner, having sold it to a group of employees in 1914.

Reproduced in 2020 by The Press of Ill Repute and ¡Viva Mexico! from the original 1910 publication.
Notes by The Press of Ill Repute are copyrighted ©2020.
All rights reserved.

ISBN: 978-1946341051 (print), 978-1946341068 (digital)

Wholesale order inquiries: chicastj@protonmail.com

Any representative of the Southern Pacific Traffic Department noted below will be pleased, on application, to furnish further information about Hermosillo, Mexico, including railway rates and service:

E. O. McCormick, Vice-President..San Francisco, Cal.
Chas. S. Fee, Passenger Traffic Manager ....San Francisco, Cal.
Jas. Horsburgh, Jr., General Passenger Agent ....San Francisco, Cal.
T. A. Graham, Ass't. General Passenger Agent, 600 South Spring St..........Los Angeles, Cal.
R. S. Stubbs, Assistant General Passenger Agent...Tucson, Ariz.
Wm. McMurray, General Passenger Agent, Oregon Lines........................Portland, Ore.
R. B. Miller, Traffic Manager, Oregon & Washington R. R.....................Portland, Ore.
W. D. Skinner, General Pass. & Fr't. Ag't., Oregon & Washington R. R..........Seattle, Wash.
D. E. Burley, General Passenger Agent, Lines East of Sparks...............Salt Lake City, Utah
Thos. J. Anderson, General Passenger Agent, G. H. & S. A. Ry................Houston, Texas
J. H. R. Parsons, Gen. Pass. Agt., M. L. & T. R. R. & S. S. Co............New Orleans, La.
R. S. Stubbs, General Pass. & Fr't. Ag't., Arizona Eastern R. R.................Tucson, Ariz.
H. Lawton, Gen. Pass. & Fr't. Ag't., Sonora Ry. and Sou. Pac. of Mexico.......Guaymas, Mex.
A. J. Dutcher, General Agent ....121 Peachtree Street, Atlanta, Ga.
W. B. Johnson, Agent...Piper Building, Baltimore Md.
J. H. Glynn, New England Agent................................170 Washington Street, Boston, Mass.
F. D. Wilson, D. P. & F. Agent, O. S. L. R. R..........................2 N. Main St., Butte, Mont.
W. G. Neimyer, General Agent..............................120 Jackson Boulevard, Chicago, Ill.
W. H. Connor, General Agent..............................53 East Fourth Street, Cincinnati, Ohio
........., General Agent ....305 Williamson Building, Cleveland, Ohio
W. K. McAllister, General Agent ....313 Railway Exchange Building, Denver, Col.
J. W. Turtle, Traveling Passenger Agent ....310 W. 5th Street, Des Moines, Iowa
J. C. Ferguson, General Agent..11 Fort Street, Detroit, Mich.
W. C. McCormick, General Agent, G. H. & S. A. Ry......................El Paso, Texas
H. G. Kaill, General Agent.......................................901 Walnut Street, Kansas City, Mo.
C. W. Mount, D. P. A., O. R. & N. Co..Lewiston, Idaho
W. E. Barnes, General Agent...............................Ave. 5 de Mayo 6B, Mexico City, Mex.
H. F. Carter, District Passenger Agent............................21 S. Third Street, Minneapolis, Minn.
L. H. Nutting, Gen. East'n Pass. Agt.,.....1 & 366 & 1158 Broadway, New York, N. Y.
J. C. Percival, Agent...Percivals Dock, Olympia, Washington
R. J. Smith, Agent...632 Chestnut Street, Philadelphia, Pa.
G. G. Herring, General Agent...............................539 Smithfield St, Pittsburg, Pa.
E. E. Ellis, General Agent, Oregon & Washington R. R..........608 First Ave., Seattle, Wash.
D. R. Gray, District Fr't. and Pass. Ag't.....................156 Main Street, Salt Lake City, Utah
W. R. Skey, Trav. Pass. Ag't., O. R. & N. Co............426 Riverside Ave., Spokane, Wash.
J. G. Lowe, General Agent..903 Olive Street, St. Louis, Mo.
F. T. Brooks, New York State Agent.....................212 W. Washington Street, Syracuse, N. Y.
Robert Lee, Gen'l. Ag't., Oregon & Washington R. R. . Eleventh & Pacific Ave., Tacoma, Wash.
A. J. Poston, Gen. Ag't., Wash. Sunset Route...................905 F Street, Washington, D. C.
Rudolph Falck, General European Passenger Agent, Amerikahaus, 25, 27 Ferdinand Strasse, Hamburg, Germany; 49 Leadenhall Street, London, E. C., England; 22 Cockspur Street, London, England; 25 Water Street, Liverpool, England; 118 Wynhaven S. S., Rotterdam, Netherlands; 11 Rue des Peignes, Antwerp, Belgium; 39 Rue St. Augustin, Paris, France.

Or Sunset Magazine Homeseekers' Bureau of Information

Portland, Oregon   San Francisco, California   Los Angeles, California

IF YOU WANT TO KEEP IN TOUCH with the growth and development of the Pacific Coast Country, read the Magazine of the Pacific and of all the Far West. It contains each month, beautifully illustrated descriptive articles and snappy stories all breathing the atmosphere of the Golden West.

Your newsdealer carries it at 15c per copy, or you can receive it every month for the next year by sending $1.50, and if you do it now, you will also receive two colored pictures of famous California Missions.

SUNSET MAGAZINE

313 Battery Street   San Francisco, California

In the Region of Hermosillo Mexico

By
Bourdon Wilson

Issued by
Sunset Magazine Homeseekers' Bureau
San Francisco, California
REISSUED & ANNOTATED IN 2020 BY THE PRESS OF ILL REPUTE
AS PART OF THE ¡VIVA MEXICO! SERIES

View of Hermosillo

Typical Mexicans and Orange Grove

BRING to your mind the black prairie soil of Illinois, the wheat lands of the Dakotas, the orange groves of Florida, the rich Yazoo-Mississippi Delta, and the black canefields of Louisiana. Then think of a million and a half acres as rich as any of these, in a land where wintry winds never blow and frost rarely ever is seen, where malaria and kindred ills are unknown and disease germs cannot exist; a million and a half acres upon every acre of which the corn of Illinois, the wheat of the Dakotas, the oranges of Florida, the cotton of the Yazoo, and the sugar-cane of Louisiana, all will grow and attain to a perfection of growth and production unsurpassed; an empire where the apple and the pineapple may be grown side by side, the grape and the grapefruit, the banana and the pear, the lime and the apricot, the guava and the nectarine, the fig and the peach; in brief, where every food-plant for man or beast, every grain and fruit and berry and vegetable of the temperate zone, as well as many of those of the tropics, will grow and bring forth their bounty with unfailing regularity. And this in a land where a man of whatsoever race or color he may be, can work out of doors every day in the year without danger of either frost-bite or sunstroke. This is the Region of Hermosillo in the fertile state of Sonora, Mexico.

Plaza and Cathedral at Hermosillo

Rubber and Banana Trees, Hermosillo

HERMOSILLO, MEXICO.

LOCATION AND DESCRIPTION

As the crow flies this land of delights lies two hundred miles south of Tucson, Arizona, and above it waves the tri-colored flag of Mexico, for it is in the Mexican State of Sonora. To get here, you may take any route you please to either El Paso, Texas, or Los Angeles, California, whence the Southern Pacific Railroad in trains of modern Pullmans and day coaches will bring you into its very heart.

Bordering in the west on the blue waters of the Gulf of California, in a broad plain, level as a floor, it slopes upward imperceptibly fifty miles or more to the east, where finger-like chains of mountains run down into it from north and south, dividing it into the valleys of the Bacuachi, the San Miguel, the Sonora, the Poza, and the Palma, in which it rises to an elevation above sea-level of 1,000 feet where the mountains wall it in on its eastern edge. These water-courses all traverse its entire length from east to west, supplying water for irrigation and other purposes. Still in a state of wildness for much the greater part, its emerald green nevertheless is dotted here and there by the gleaming white buildings of an *hacienda* (farm), surrounded by broad fields and growing crops; and in its center stands the capital city of the state, Hermosillo.

ITS CLIMATE

Winter, meaning the colder season, comes during the months of December and January, when the thermometer now and then sinks to the freezing point and a light frost or two comes in the more elevated part east of Hermosillo; but in its meaning of the season, when plant growth is suspended, it comes in April, May and June, for during these months rain rarely ever falls and the streams all but run dry, wherefore the face of the earth turns brown. February, March and a part of April, form the delightful spring season, during which the thermometer ranges between 65° and 75°. Summer, meaning the warmer season, begins in April and continues till October, when the weather cools very perceptibly into fall. While summer here is longer than in the northern half of the United States, it is not so oppressive, for the days are much shorter and the nights longer, giving the earth time in which to cool off once in every twenty-four hours; moreover, in the bone-dry air that prevails during all but July, August and September, which months constitute what is termed the rainy season, the perceptible heat is at least fifteen degrees less than in the humid Eastern States. In other words, with the thermometer standing at 90° both here and in, say, Ohio or Mississippi, one feels fifteen degrees cooler here than there.

The average annual rainfall is about that of many highly productive sections in Southern California. For the ten years from 1900 to 1909, this average ran from 6 inches to 24.12, the average for the ten years being 11.43. Besides that, as nearly all of it comes during July,

Flood Water Irrigation

August and September, when earth and air are at their hottest, much the greater part of it is immediately absorbed by the eager plant growth, which at once springs up to cover the earth with its greenery, instead of escaping again into the air by means of evaporation, as in other irrigated parts of the world where it comes at a season when it is too cold for seeds to germinate. In other words, one inch of rain here is worth as much to the farmer as two, if not three, in Colorado and California. To complete the picture, it must be added that, during the ten years already given, rain did not fall on more than four days in succession at any time, which is to say that the long wet spells sometimes so disastrous to the farmer in the eastern United States are unknown here. The ground seldom ever gets so wet that plowing cannot be resumed within twenty-four hours after the rain stops falling, owing to the sandy porous nature of the land; and, as has been seen, the rains cease altogether before even the quickest growing crop reaches maturity, which assures dry weather for harvesting.

As to healthfulness, it is easy to understand why a country which is practically without rain for nine months of the year, and which, therefore, escapes the contamination of decaying vegetation, should be free from the ills consequent thereto; and it is equally easy of comprehension that one need have no fear of disease germs in a country where the sun shines at least a part of practically every day in the year, and where one may literally live out of doors all the time.

THE SOIL

In ancient times this was a part of the Gulf of California, which has been filled in during the slow progress of the centuries by wash from the mountains, disintegrated rock, sand and decayed forest growth, which year by year mingled with the vegetation of the lowlands, forming a loose sandy soil of unsurpassed richness, and bottomless, so far as plant life is concerned. Every year, with the coming of the summer overflow of the streams, from one quarter to an inch of silt, rich and black, is added wherever the water settles, and wherever water is put on the land for irrigation, thus annually renewing the soil.

IRRIGATION METHODS

There are in vogue here three methods of irrigating the land. First, turning on of the water from a ditch; second, the bolsa or check system; and third, the utilization of the flood waters of the several streams. The first and second of these are too familiar to require description here, but the third is peculiar. A few miles below Hermosillo, where the mountains stop and what is styled the Delta begins, the earth becomes so flat that the streams no longer have beds, but instead spread their waters out thinly over a vast area of country. And here, by means of low embankments thrown up across the flow, the water is diverted to the land to be irrigated. This is, however, only wet weather irrigation, and therefore will be referred to again under the heading of dry farming.

1000-Acre Field of Young Corn

While enough rain falls here and in the surrounding mountains to irrigate fully the entire section under discussion, by far the greater part of it now is allowed to go to waste. But, as there are many fine sites for reservoirs, this will be remedied as the demand for land grows till all is utilized. And besides water from this source, much will be obtained from surface wells, as it is found at a very shallow depth, from one and a half to six feet, over certain large areas; especially is this true of parts of the Poza, the Sonora, and the Bacuache valleys, and the great plain bordered by the Gulf of California. Moreover, this is a vast artesian basin in which flowing wells already have been struck at a depth of 450 feet and over; the railroad's well at Pasquiera, which is 460 feet in depth, flows 3,600 gallons per hour.

FARMING

Cotton is, perhaps, the greatest money producer of all the many staple crops which may be grown here, and this in spite of the presence of the picudo, or boll weevil. Planted in April, to bring the fruit to maturity immediately after the rainy season, and irrigated throughout the period of its growth, it will bring, on the greater part of the land under consideration, from one and a half to two bales to the acre— bales of the standard weight of 500 pounds each. This for the ordinary short staple varieties; while soil and climatic conditions here closely parellel those of Egypt no experiments have yet been made with Egyptian cotton. Experience has taught, however, that cotton planted in April and irrigated, is subjected to attack by the boll weevil, and therefore may not be grown in this manner for more than four or five years in succession, when its planting must be discontinued for an equal length of time, to let the weevil die out. To plant at the beginning of the rainy season, and then refrain from irrigating the crop, would be, perhaps, the more profitable practice in the long run, although the yield in lint might not exceed one bale to the acre, for it has been demonstrated that the weevil requires moisture if it is to accomplish much harm. The land being cleaned off early in the year, and all the refuse burned, the weevil's eggs will hatch during the warm March and April days, the season of brownness, during which the insect can find nothing upon which to subsist or in which to lay its eggs; and it will be killed by the extremely dry weather following in May and June. As all cotton planters know, to plant at a season when the nights are hot and rains are certain, assures the most rapid growth of which the plant is capable, wherefore the picking of cotton planted in July may be expected to begin almost as early as that planted in April. This shortening of the growing season means a lessened expense for cultivation, as there is no crab-grass to fight here, only cockle-burs and "careless" weeds, and in some places morning glories. Moreover, with the bolls opening after the rains have ceased, and with no winds to whip the cotton out on the ground, it may be allowed to remain on the stalks much longer than elsewhere; indeed, there have been instances where the entire crop

Cutting Wheat

was gathered at one picking and without material loss. Everything considered, cotton may be produced here for one-half the cost of its production in the most favored parts of the United States. And, as there is a high import duty on cotton brought into Mexico, and the consumption at the present time is twice as great as the production, the prices here range in the neighborhood of two cents higher than in the United States.

Wheat comes next in the list of money-makers. This crop usually follows one of corn or beans in the same year, wherefore it is planted from October to February. Its yield is from twenty to seventy bushels to the acre, and all that now is grown here finds a ready home market at from $2.00 to $2.25 the hundred pounds.

Garbanza is a close competitor with wheat and cotton as a profitable field crop. It is a plant of the pea kind, and is highly valued in both Mexico and Spain as a staple article of food. Its culture is the same as that of beans, and its average yield per acre is about 1,900 pounds, which will bring at present prices from $50.00 to $60.00. As with wheat, garbanza may be grown as a second crop.

Corn produces from forty to eighty bushels to the acre, though as high as one hundred and twenty have been grown with careful cultivation on some of the richest spots. Planted in July its growth is so rapid that it requires very little cultivation, and it sells readily at from $1.00 to $1.10 the hundred pounds, shelled.

Beans, or *frijoles*, as their excellence has caused them to become known around the world, are planted in August, and again as a winter crop. Their yield is from twenty-five to fifty bushels to the acre, and they sell readily at about $3.50 the hundred pounds.

Barley is planted in the fall and winter, and the yield is from forty to eighty bushels to the acre.

Oats are not much in favor, though the yield is high. On the lands irrigated by flood water, the oat is regarded as a pest, as it easily shells out here, permitting the water to carry it everywhere and mix it with other crops.

Cow peas are not grown here to any great extent, although their growth and yield are magnificent.

Tobacco is known to grow well in the eastern part of this section, where much is profitably produced for home consumption.

Sugar-cane flourishes here. From a piece of land three hundred feet square 150,000 pounds of cane were cut last year. Concrete figures of its yield in sugar are not obtainable, for the cane here is regarded as a confection, wherefore much of the crop now grown is sold in the stalk, in the local markets and in the large mining camps of Sonoma and Southern Arizona.

Sweet potatoes yield enormously, specimens of the red varieties weighing twenty-three pounds having been grown.

Family Orchard—Peach and Nectarine Trees

Irish potatoes do not do so well as in some parts of the United States, and therefore are grown only in the kitchen and truck gardens.

Milo maize and Egyptian corn are exactly suited to the soil and climate, and therefore grow and yield well. Sorghum, peanuts and broomcorn, all may be grown with profit. And the same will undoubtedly be found true of flax and buckwheat.

The production of henequin, or sisal, and other members of the agave family, all valuable for their fiber, is still in the experimental stage.

Tomatoes begin to ripen here in February. As the yield is large they may be grown very profitably for shipment to the United States.

Canteloupes begin to ripen the last week in April, wherefore they also are to be grown with much profit.

Watermelons yield equally well. From 6,000 plants twenty-eight carloads were picked and shipped to Arizona and New Mexico points last season, where they brought their owner $10,000.

Alfalfa yields five crops of hay each year, the total annual cut being about an average of six tons to the acre. Baled, it finds a ready home market at from $12.50 to $20.00 the ton.

Onions, celery, asparagus, cabbage, and all the other vegetables of the temperate zone, grow finely, though it must be left to future experimentation to decide which of them may be grown with profit for the export markets.

The same is to be said of strawberries, blackberries, raspberries and dewberries, all of which bring heavy crops of finely flavored fruit with never failing regularity.

FRUIT-GROWING

While all of the deciduous fruits will grow here, apples, peaches, pears, plums, nectarines, apricots, etc., it cannot be stated that they will do as well as in the United States, for this is a little too far south for them, especially apples. Just what they will do has not yet been ascertained; while every *hacendado* (farmer) has his family orchard containing specimens of some or all of these trees, his efforts at fruit production, like those of the great mass of his brethren in the United States, ended with the putting out of the trees, they being left to fight for themselves except for the irrigation given them from time to time. However, basing upon the fruits thus produced, it may be stated as a fact that all may be grown for home uses, while experimentation and proper care of the trees may develop that some can be grown for the market with profit.

Grapes do splendidly here, and future experimentation will reveal that they may be grown with large profit.

It is of interest to note that the persimmon which grows wild all over the southern United States, here bears fruit as large as apples, though the flavor is not quite so good.

Graded Cattle—Hacienda "Europa"

Dates grow and ripen here as well as anywhere in the world, and in the course of time will become a profitable crop for export.

Olives and figs both do well. While it has been ascertained that pineapples, bananas, guavas, and other tropical fruits will grow here, it has not been developed that they may be profitably grown for market.

Citrus fruits find here a soil and climate exactly suited to the perfection of their growth, wherefore Hermosillo oranges are noted far and wide for their sweetness and exquisite flavor. Owing to the import duty placed upon them by the United States, they are much less known there than in Canada, to which country nearly the entire crop is shipped every year, where they are in great favor, although all are of the old unimproved seed variety. From the viewpoint of the California and Florida grower, no care is taken of the groves for the greater part, except to irrigate them, nevertheless their owners find them highly profitable. However, progressive growers have begun putting out groves of Washington navels and other improved kinds, and pruning and spraying and cultivating the trees properly; and, as the fruit ripens sweet here a month earlier than in either California or Florida, it is safe to predict that Hermosillo oranges will begin to fight their way in large numbers into the United States during the next few years, in spite of the tariff wall. Nearly four hundred cars of oranges were shipped from Hermosillo last year.

The Sicilian and all other kinds of lemons do as well here as oranges. And the same is to be said of the lime, both the sweet and the sour kinds.

DRY FARMING

It is doubtful if any other part of the world offers the dry farmer such wonderful advantages as he finds here. As has already been stated, practically all of the rainfall comes when earth and air are at their warmest, when seeds sprout and spring up into growing plants within three or four days after planting, absorbing in their growth moisture much of which is lost by evaporation in other countries, where the rains come in the cold season. Moreover, much of the land can be thoroughly soaked at least once every summer by the flood waters from the streams. There is no reason why all of the crops known to this section should not be grown profitably in this manner. So far there has been very little dry farming done here, but an experimental farm has been established, near Hermosillo, which is being watched with no small interest.

STOCK-RAISING

This is a country of luxuriant growth of nutritious native grasses, which is to say that it is a natural stock country. And when it is added that these grasses cure themselves into quite good hay, upon which animals make their living throughout the year, it is to say that

"On the Y," Where the

Shipping Scene at Guaymas

Road Enters Hermosillo

Palma Valley—From the Hill of Windows

Views of Hacienda "La Labor," Senora Mexico
House and Chapel
Colonnade Porch
Servants' Quarters

it is a highly profitable one. Thousands of both horses and cattle are owned and ranged here and in the surrounding mountains, to say nothing of the lowly—but in Mexico, profitable—goat.

While the horses are almost all of the wiry mustang breed, a determined effort to improve them has recently started, bringing in numerous thoroughbred stallions of the Percheron, Clydesdale, and other breeds. And while the long horn of the old style Texas steer still dominates the great herds of cattle, the white face of the graded Hereford, the black and white of the Holstein, and the red of the Durham, are seen on every hand, evidence that many thoroughbred bulls of these breeds have been imported during recent years. Hogs are not raised in large numbers, in spite of the fact that it would be highly profitable to do so, as the hog is remarkably free from disease here. In common with his scrub brother, it has been proved that the Angora goat can be raised here with large profit, wherefore their number is being rapidly increased.

LAND AND LAND VALUES

But little more than two per cent of the arable land in this section now is under cultivation; which is to say that there is room here for a farming population a thousand times as large as at present. The titles to most of it are good, or at least may be easily perfected, nevertheless the incoming American settler should look carefully to this. The value of the land depends very largely on the water rights pertaining to it, though existing improvements, nearness to markets and transportation facilities and fertility, have their bearing upon it here as elsewhere. The wild lands may be bought for as low as $5.00 an acre, without water for irrigation; and wild land in the Delta section, but which may be flooded by overflow water, for as low as $10.00; whereas lands of the same quality, but with water available from permanent ditches are held at from $50.00 to $150.00.

While none of the land here can be classed as wooded in the sense of having merchantable timber upon it, practically all of it has a growth of such trees as the mesquite, ironwood and palo verde, which make lasting posts and excellent firewood.

LABOR CONDITIONS

The Yaqui Indians have performed much of the labor of this region ever since its first settlement by white men, and this in spite of the fact that the tribe has been almost constantly at war with the government during all of that time. Occupying from time immemorial the Yaqui Valley in the south, there bidding defiance to both state and national authority, from time to time they would issue forth to work or to murder as the whim seized them.

But in 1902 the federal government decided to put an end to this state of affairs, and captured and punished some of the murderers. Then flamed out the war by which this region was devastated for the six years following. At all times it was within the power of the govern-

Hacienda "Molino de Camou"

Flour Mill—Hacienda "Europa"

ment to end this war by the simple method, so familiar to American frontiersmen, of exterminating the Indians, but it chose instead the slower but more humane deportation of the irreconcilables, as they were captured, to far away Yucatan, whence they were not likely to find their way back. That they were not furnished Pullman cars in which to travel, or feather beds upon which to sleep, is a fact; but neither were the Chiricahua Apaches when the United States, in 1886, deported the irreconcilables of that murderous tribe from Arizona to far away Florida. Both steps were wholly justifiable, for the one made possible the civilization of the white man in Arizona, and the other now has done the same in the region of Hermosillo. With the Yaquis scattered, and their fighting power crushed as completely as the Americans crushed that of the Sioux and Apaches, there is no reason why this region should not now increase in both population and prosperity by leaps and bounds. While there is a scarcity of labor here at present, owing to the deportation of the Yaquis, this will be remedied, as the demand grows, by bringing laborers from the states further south, where there is a surplus. As this inevitable influx of labor from the more southerly districts is attracted into the Hermosillo region and begins to supply the now existing demand for men to carry on the work of tilling, sowing and harvesting the rich crops possible in this fertile region, capital must as inevitably find a constantly increasing lure for profitable investment in agricultural, industrial and commercial projects.

Picnic Scene—Mexicans of the Better Class

Thriving Sonora Poultry

THE PEOPLE HERE AND THE LAWS

No American or European need be afraid to come to Mexico, for both life and property are as secure in all parts of the Republic as in any part of the United States. While Americans will find the laws in many respects different from their own, and therefore somewhat irksome at first, they are just laws in the main, and suited to the conditions here. No self-respecting man or woman, who also respects the rights and sensibilities of others, need be afraid of not getting along with the Mexicans; they are warm-hearted, generous, and hospitable to the last degree. Many of them in this region have traveled or been educated in the United States, and therefore understand American ways; and a considerable percentage of the population here speaks English, which language now is being taught in the public schools. They dress here exactly as Americans dress; and they read the American newspapers, which enables them to discuss American affairs intelligently. Their homes are furnished in good taste, and their manners are the manners of well-bred people the world over. In other words, they are a people among whom you can soon make yourself feel perfectly at home. And besides the native population, there now are about five hundred Americans resident in this region, where they are engaged in farming, mining, stock-raising, etc. Nobody here cares what your religion is, or how or when or where you worship; and in the towns you will find good public schools.

RAILROADS AND SEAPORTS

The Southern Pacific Company's main line from Los Angeles, California, to the City of Mexico, traverses the heart of this region, giving first-class passenger service to both the United States and Southern Mexico, and also the best of shipping facilities. A concession has been granted for the construction of a railway from Ures on the Sonora

Retail Stores in Hermosillo

Wholesale Dry Goods House

Modern Business Office, Hermosillo

River, via Hermosillo, to Kino Bay on the Gulf of California, where it is planned to establish a seaport. At present Guaymas is the one seaport town of this region, and here come vessels from all parts of the world.

MANUFACTORIES

All of the manufacturing industries of this region are located in the city of Hermosillo, under which heading they will be set forth, excepting only the cotton mill in the town of Los Angeles. This mill makes the coarser grades of cotton cloth, its capacity is one hundred bales of cotton per month.

THE CITY OF HERMOSILLO

Literally translated, Hermosillo means "the little beautiful one," and it is not a misnomer in this instance, for it is a place both beautiful and picturesque. It is situated on the Sonora River, nor far from the center of the region to which it gives a name. Like other Mexican cities, it centers about a plaza, or public park, the Plaza Zaragoza, on opposite sides of which stand the Cathedral and the State Capitol. The population of the city is about 14,000. It has electric lights and power, water works, and bonds have been sold for the purpose of installing a modern sewer system, work upon which will soon begin. Nearly all of the streets are macadamized, with cement sidewalks; and while most of them are narrow, from the American viewpoint, they are serviceable as well as picturesque. Most of the houses are of the flat-roofed Mexican style, with stern exterior, but many of them made beautiful within by a *patio*, or courtyard, set with flowers and ornamental trees. Besides the Plaza Zaragoza, the Parque Ramon Corral with its broad acres of orange grove and flowers and ornamental trees, named in honor of the republic's vice-president, affords a place for rest and recreation. Seen from a distance, the city appears to be trying to hide itself in the beautiful orange groves amid which it is set.

Besides being the place of residence of most of the well-to-do people of this region, Hermosillo is a manufacturing city. Here are located three flour mills, one of them with a capacity of four hundred barrels per day; a large match factory, a cracker factory, a foundry and machine shop, three tanneries, two ice manufactories, a modern well-equipped brewery, a broom factory, two manufactories of preserves and other sweets, a packing-house and cold-storage plant, which supplies meats for all the country about, a macaroni factory, several small shoe factories, and several establishments for the manufacture of all kinds of ready-made clothing, from both Mexican and foreign cloths. It is also a financial center for here are located four banks, all of them strong financial institutions. Furthermore, a concession has been granted for the establishment of a Mortgage-Loan Bank here, the ample capital for which has already been fully subscribed. This bank will lend money to landowners for the purpose of developing their properties.

State Capitol, Hermosillo

Sonora River—Near Hermosillo

Luxuriant Growth of Date Palms

Orange Grove, Hermosillo

Wild Native Grasses

Hermosillo is a commercial city, with several large wholesale houses, which supply the trade not only of this region, but of the vast country east and south as well. Its retail stores of all kinds would be a credit to any American city of 100,000 people. Upon their shelves are to be found every article of manufacture known in the United States, not only those of Mexican make, but, as well, those of American, English, French, German, Italian, etc. Of especial interest to the intending settler here are the various houses which deal in farming implements and machinery, of which they now are selling five or six carloads per month.

There is a good opening in Hermosillo for a small but up-to-date American daily newspaper, giving the press dispatches. It would have the enthusiastic support of the entire American population, and that of the Mexicans who read English, while all the merchants could readily be brought to see the value of advertising. The five papers now published here are all weeklies, and printed in Spanish. And a first-class cannery here would pay well, as would an American bakery. But above all, a good creamery is needed, for there is none in this region, wherefore high prices are paid for butter imported from Kansas City.

As a winter resort, Hermosillo stands preeminent, for the winter climate here can be described only as delicious; it is never hot, and never cold, there are no winds to annoy, and the sun shines brilliantly every day. Moreover, there are good hotels, two of them conducted by Americans as American hotels, where one may obtain all of the comforts and many of the luxuries of hotel life. Those traveling to or from California via the Southern or Sunset routes, if a few days time can be spared, by all means should break their journey at Tucson and take a side-trip to Hermosillo. The run down occupies less than ten hours, and can be made in modern Pullman sleepers, which run through from Los Angeles, California. A very low rate of fare is given to all who take this trip.

Come and see for yourselves what a lovely and magnificent country this is.

Note.—If not otherwise stated, all of the values given in the foregoing are expressed in American money.

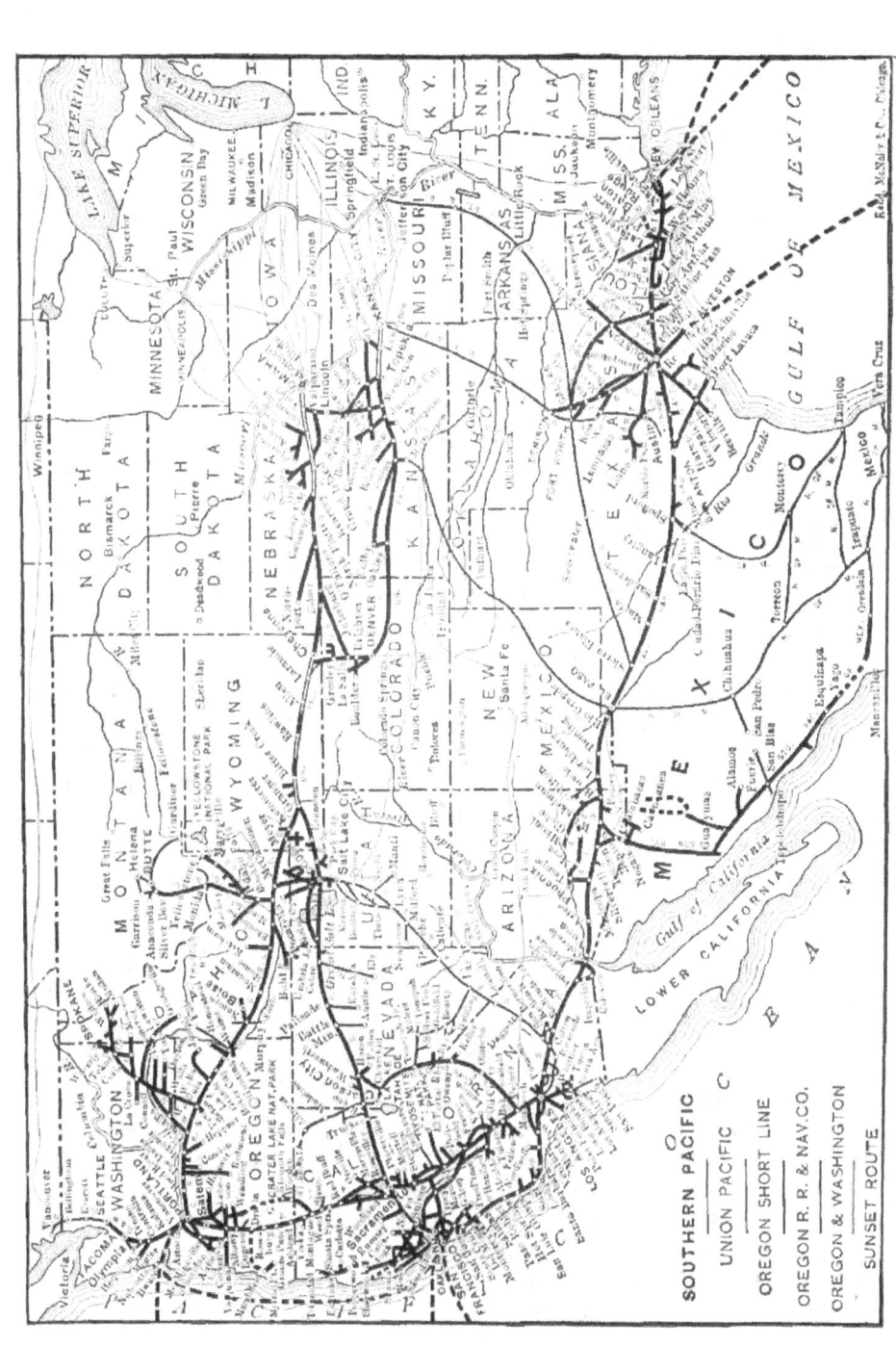

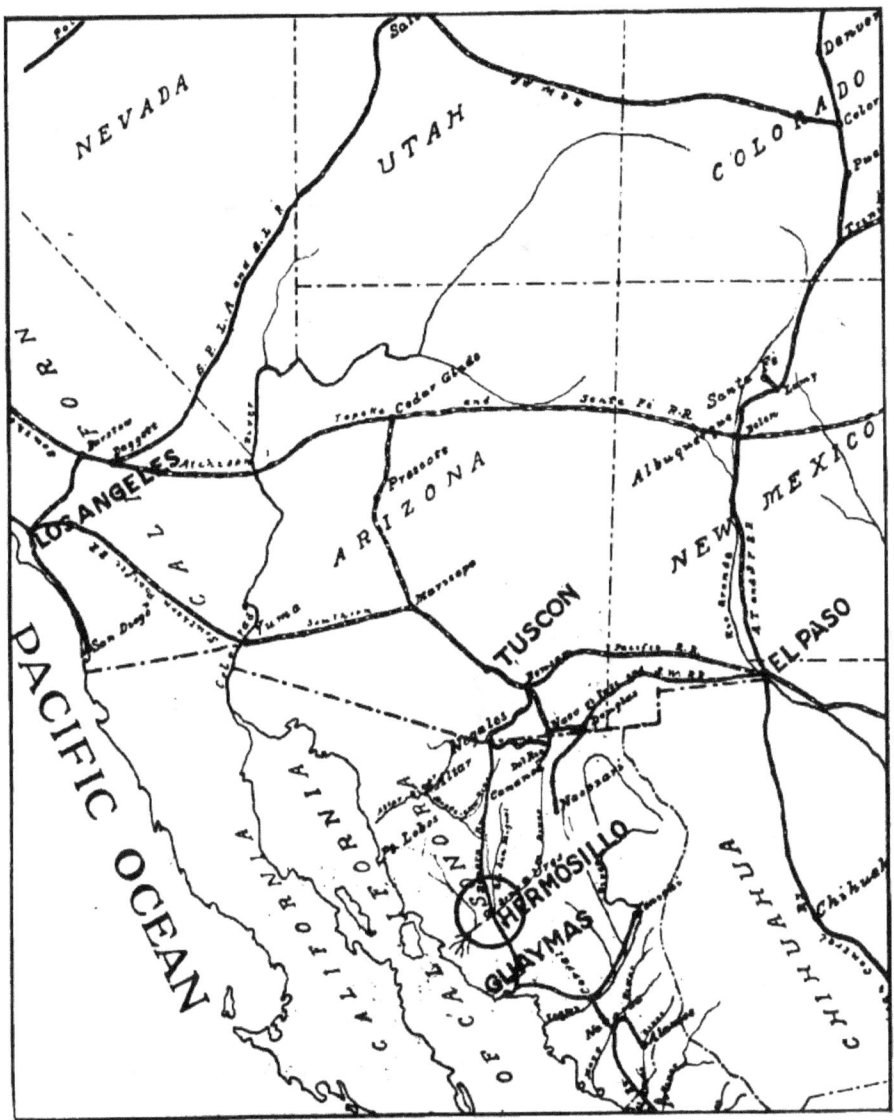

Hermosillo, the New Dixie Land

A vast tract of rich cotton land just being opened to settlement and within a few hours of Tucson, Arizona. Here land costs from five to ten dollars and yields two bales of cotton to the acre.

The side trip from Tucson to Hermosillo will amply repay the seeker for wealth, health and scenic beauty.

Sunset Homeseekers' Bureau of Information

Governor **Alberto Cubillas** of the State of *Sonora, Mexico*, writes as follows from the State Capitol at

Hermosillo

CORRESPONDENCIA PARTICULAR
DEL GOBERNADOR
DEL ESTADO DE SONORA

CAMARA DE COMERCIO,
      Hermosillo.

Gentlemen:-

    I have observed with great pleasure the movement you have instituted of advertising Hermosillo and the surrounding country in foreign periodicals, and take this opportunity of assuring you that your efforts in this direction have the hearty support of both the Federal and the State Governments. You may assure such persons as your endeavors may interest, that they are welcome to our State. We have here wonderful natural resources of all kinds--agricultural, mineral, etc.--and we need a healthy immigration of sober, industrious people to help develop them.

    I am writing this letter in English, so that you may use it in your publicity-work if you deem it convenient.

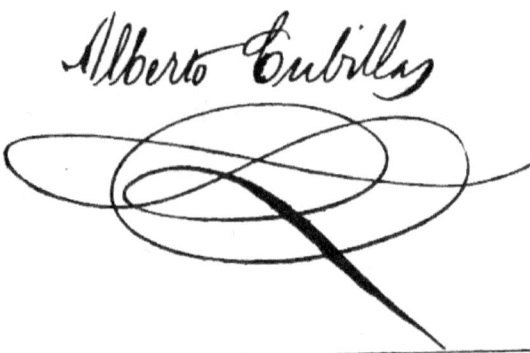

This assurance of the hearty support of the State and Federal Governments for the movement that has been instituted by the business men of HERMOSILLO, together with the response that has already met our efforts to bring live hustling new-comers to this section, make us doubly sure that this will indeed be a Happy New Year for us. In this cheerful frame of mind, we wish all of you whose eyes may fall on this page, a very Happy New Year, and we add the suggestion that the best way for you to make it both Happy and Prosperous, is to COME TO HERMOSILLO. Write and we'll tell you why. Address *Secretary, CAMARA DE COMERCIO (Chamber of Commerce), Hermosillo, Sonora, Mexico.* Illustrated booklet for the asking.

Additional Tidbits of Interest

ADDED BY THE PRESS OF ILL REPUTE

left page: Letter from the Governor of Sonora in support of the promotional efforts of Sunset and welcoming visitors and settlers.

this page: Advertisement for land in Sonora, Mexico, in January 1911 issue of Sunset.

following pages: Short story by Bourdon Wilson, published in 1899.

Sunset Homeseekers' Bureau of Information

The Sonora Delta Land Company *of* MEXICO

PIONEERS of the land business in Sonora, are offering rich Delta lands in tracts of from 160 to 100,000 acres, in the FAMOUS SONORA RIVER VALLEY, situated near Hermosillo, the Capital City, and only a few miles from Southern Pacific R. R. of Mexico. *Splendid markets for everything.* Settlers coming every day. *Remember this* is your last opportunity to get a fine piece of land for little money.

EASY TERMS. BUY BEFORE THE RISE IN PRICE.

Send for illustrated booklet to 942-1 Phelan Bldg., San Francisco, or Hermosillo, Sonora, Mexico. We own and control over 500,000 acres on the West Coast in Sonora.

A MEXICAN CONJUGATION OF THE VERB "TO LOVE."

By Bourdon Wilson.

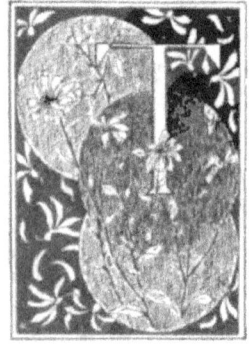

To those of its inhabitants who claimed the Castilian as their mother tongue, the little town of flat-roofed adobe houses was known as La Villa Rica del Valle. To its dwellers of Anglo-Saxon origin it was known simply as Rica; while to those of whatever race or tongue who did not dwell therein, it was scarcely known at all. For, shut in by ranges of lofty, forbidding mountains, and weary leagues of desert sand, its existence was unsuspected by the world beyond, save by "Uncle Sam," who had established a post office within its walls. Its population, which was composed almost entirely of Mexicans, was leavened by a few Americans—cattle men, the postmaster and a saloon keeper or two.

It was one evening as we (that is to say the Americans, for Mexicans unless of the fair sex did not count with us) were gathered, as usual, about the bar of the Espiritu Santo saloon, that a Mexican rushed in and breathlessly informed us that Manuel Garcia, one of the well-to-do Mexicans, and the husband of the prettiest woman in the pueblo, had stabbed his wife and made his escape. Instantly there arose a chorus of indignant exclamations and outbursts of profanity. We all knew the woman by sight, and what one of us had not violated the tenth commandment on some occasion when she had passed demurely along, on her way to mass in the half-ruined little adobe church? Our indignation quickly rose to fever heat, and someone proposed that a party start in pursuit of Garcia.

"Now you fellers are er makin' fools er yerselves," objected "Buster Bill," who had the reputation of being the best shot and hardest drinker in the pueblo. "Better jest let them greasers settle their own scraps. Besides that," he went on, "yer jest can't never tell when er woman natcherly needs knifin'."

But a few minutes later, when old "Pap" Flaxen, our host of the Espiritu Santo, hurriedly entered the barroom, and announced that his horse had been taken by Garcia, Bill brought his glass down on the bar with a crash.

"Le's hurry up, fellers, and git our hosses," he cried, excitedly, "we're er loosin' time."

Hastily we caught and saddled our horses, and with Bill in the lead, we galloped out of town in the direction Garcia had been seen to take. It was not long before the bright moonlight revealed to our watchful eyes the fresh trail of a horse that led off to the right of the trail we were following.

"He's er headin' fer th' Santy Fé trail!" our leader exclaimed, "an' if we kin beat 'im ter Crow Spring, we kin jest set down an' wait fer 'im. He's boun' ter git water there or nowhere, fer it's th' only water this side er th' Pecos. Reckin we had better try ter make it through Gringo Pass," he continued. "There ain't been much snow fell this winter, an' most likely we kin make it; at any rate, it's our best chance to ketch 'im."

Following Bill's advice, we slightly altered our course and headed straight for the mountains. The pass was found free from snow, and, as the moon sank behind a distant mountain range, we again struck into the open plain, and within a few hours arrived at the spring. The absence of any fresh trail about the place assured us that Garcia, who had gone around by the much safer but more distant Paso del Sur, had not yet arrived. We picketed our horses in a nearby arroya, where they could not be seen by the Mexican, then hid ourselves about the spring and awaited the coming of the fugitive. Daylight came and the first rays of the sun were glistening on the snowy peaks of the mountain range we had just crossed, when he came in sight. With loose-hanging bridle reins, and with a dazed, stupid look on his face, he rode fairly into the trap we had set for him. We covered him with our rifles, and Bill ordered him to halt and dismount. Pale and trembling, he silently obeyed. Then his dull look of misery gave way to one of more intelligence, as his gaze passed from one face to another.

"*Por el amor de Dios, Señores*," he gasped; "tell me quickly—is she dead?"

"Not yet," Bill replied; "but 'tain't *yore* fault she ain't."

"Thank God!" cried Garcia, fervently; "I hope she won't die—*a Dios!* I hope she won't!"

"Oughter felt that way before you done it," Bill curtly replied.

"What made yer do it, Manuel?" asked "Kid" Flaxen, old Pap's son, who was more or less intimate with the Mexicans of the pueblo.

"Yes," added Bill, who was in high good humor, now that the criminal was in his clutches; "set down here and tell us erbout it. 'Twa'n't er bit like yer ter go an' steal er hoss."

The Mexican seated himself on the ground, and we gathered about him, eager to hear his story. He seemed in an almost exhausted condition, and Kid handed him a large bottle of whiskey he had taken from his pocket. Garcia drank deeply, and passed the bottle to Bill, who was anxiously awaiting his turn.

"Now shoot out, Manuel, and tell us how you come ter do it," said Kid, in a sympathetic tone. "Yer don't look like er man who'd hit er woman."

"Nor steal er hoss, neither," added Bill.

"No, señor—*por Dios*, no!" Manuel exclaimed, giving Kid a grateful look. "By the Holy Mary, I swear that I never laid hand on a woman before. Much as I have been provoked, I never struck her. What happened yesterday was the affair of a moment. Insane with rage and jealousy, I drew my knife, and the next thing I knew I was galloping away, feeling that I had stabbed somebody."

"An' stoled somebody's hoss," Bill added, dryly.

"No, señor, I would have sent it back."

"Ah!" ejaculated Bill; but the sarcasm implied by the tone of his voice was lost upon the prisoner.

"Listen, gentlemen," Manuel continued, "and I will tell you. The woman I hurt, as you know, is my wife; I have never had a thought for any woman but her. Madly and foolishly have I loved her, for she is cold-hearted, and has never loved me in return. Before our marriage it was her

"'A DIOS, MANUELITO!' SHE CRIED, WITH A LITTLE SHRIEK, 'I KNEW YOU WOULD COME BACK.'"

delight to see me furious with jealousy, and three times our engagement was broken. I fought a duel each time. But as often as it was broken my love for her would overpower me, and drag me back to her feet, her abject slave.

Finally we were married, and I was mad with joy and happiness, and acted in such a way that my friends made fun of me. I saw it, but heeded it not, so great was my delight at getting Josefa. When the holy father, Geronimo, proclaimed us man and wife, and with outstretched hands gave us his benediction, I thought my troubles were over. *A Dios!* but it was not so. When you are married, señores," he went on, "you will know what a hold a wife has on a man, especially if he loves her to distraction and never looks at another woman.

"I can't deny, señores," he continued, "that I have an evil temper, which at times overleaps all control, but she was a devil, señores, to have so provoked me. She knew she could do what she pleased with me, and began a systematic course of tyranny over me, and I soon found myself hating her oftener than I loved her. As often as my heart would melt with tenderness and love she would repel my advances with coldness and scorn, and maybe arouse the devil within me with praises of other men—those who had been my rivals. It was on such occasions, señores, that my hand, of its own volition, would seek the hilt of my knife; and why I did not kill her long ago the good God only knows. Sometimes, when I was at the worst, I have said to her, '*Cuidado,* have a care—all things have a limit!' But she would answer with taunts and jeering laughter. *A Dios!* that she had taken a little notice of her danger!"

"Yes—'twould er saved trouble an' good hoss flesh," Bill replied, unsympathetically.

"For a long time," Manuel went on, not noticing the interruption, "I resisted the promptings of the demon to sink my knife in her breast, but it came at last; and now *la probrecita* will die. And *ay de me!*" he wailed, as he leaped wildly to his feet, "it is I who killed her!"

Instantly Bill had him covered with his rifle, but remained seated, watching silently his every movement, as does the cat the mouse with which it is playing.

"Love her now, señores?" Manuel cried, his arms outstretched, and his voice rising to a shrill key. "Before God, yes; a thousand times more than before I gave her those cruel stabs. Ah, I must see her before she dies! Why did I leave her? *Querida mia,* why did I leave you? I was a coward!" he moaned, reseating himself, "and did not have the courage to face it out. But my mind was in a whirl, and my only idea was to get a horse and fly."

"Well, yer got th' hoss all right ernough—yer did fer er fack," Bill remarked, grimly.

Manuel seemed not to hear, but sat staring out across the desert with round, wide open eyes, as though trying, with all the power of his memory, to recall a scene.

Kid, who was sitting somewhat behind Bill, had been listening with breathless attention to Manuel's recital, and whenever I stole a look at his smooth, boyish face, I could see that he was not the least moved of the listeners. As Manuel became silent I noticed Kid slyly draw from his pocket a vial, from which he poured into his hand a pinch of whitish powder. Replacing the vial in his pocket, he poured the powder from his hand into the open mouth of the whiskey bottle. Then, shaking the whiskey about, thus dissolving the powder, he passed the bottle to Bill, who gave it his grateful attention. Manuel took no notice of the bottle when Bill passed it to him, much to the relief of Kid, whose eyes closely followed every movement. I pretended to take a long drink when my turn came, but in reality barely tasted the liquor, and returned the bottle to Kid. We had been in the saddle all the night before, and the loss of sleep, combined with the whiskey and the warmth of the sun, began to tell on us. Bill was soon nodding; then he sprawled over on his back and went fast asleep. I stretched out, and, while pretending to sleep, closely watched Kid's movements. A few minutes passed; then Kid rose to his feet, and going noiselessly to Manuel's side, shook him.

"Wake up, Manuel, and pull yer freight," he said, in a low tone.

"But I'm a prisoner, señor," Manuel replied, gazing questioningly into the other's face, "and must wait until you are ready to take me back to Villa Rica."

"Yer ain't no prisoner now—can't yer sabe?" said Kid, impatiently.

"But, señor," Manuel protested, "I must go back to Villa Rica, and will wait until they awake."

"Are yer plum locoed?" Kid whispered, angrily. "I doped th' liquor, and they ain't goin' ter wake before night; an' ef yer don't skip while Buster Bill's 'sleep, yer won't never git no further."

"But surely, señor, he will take me back to Villa Rica?"

"Take the devil!" exclaimed Kid. "Whoever heard of Buster Bill takin' a hoss thief any further 'n th' nearest tree? Yer er hoss thief ter him —don't yer sabe? What made yer take th' ol' man's hoss, anyhow?"

"I took the first horse I saw, and meant to send it back from Santa Fé."

"That's all right, an' I believe yer, but Bill wouldn't, an' ef he fin's yer here when he wakes, he'll shorely hang yer fer a hoss thief."

A pallor spread over Manuel's face, and Kid led him unresisting toward the horses.

"Take my hoss. I give him to yer," I heard Kid say, and then my feigned sleep became real.

We galloped back into Rica the next day, but not until we were safely within the Espiritu Santo did we tell our story. It was received in the light of a good joke on Bill, who, for the first time in his history, had permitted a horse thief to escape from his clutches.

"Must be er gettin' ready ter jine th' church, William," suggested Pap, as he shoved a bottle along the bar toward Bill.

"Jine th' devil!" Bill replied, hotly. "It was yore rank ol' taranteler juice 'at done it. I jest believe you put morphine in it, so's er feller'll go ter sleep an' think he's drunk. You fellers thinks it's mighty funny, an' 'er good joke on me, but jest let me get my hooks onter that greaser ergin!"

"Wouldn't hurt him, would yer, parson?" asked Pap. "Dock says his wife's er mendin', an' is er goin' ter git well."

"Wouldn't I hurt him?" rejoined Bill. "Why, I'd jest snake him in ter that purty wife er hisn, an' whatever she said fer me ter do ter him, that's what I'd do, ef it was ter burn 'im at th' stake!"

I had walked to the window and was looking out when I saw something that caused me to leave the room and hurriedly make my way across the bare little plaza.

"What are you doing here, Manuel?" I asked a man, who was alighting from a weary horse that I recognized as Kid Flaxen's. "Are you crazy that you can't remember what has happened?"

"What! is she dead?" he asked, turning white.

"No," I replied, "she will get well; but the horse?"

With a bound he turned and started toward the nearest house—his own, but Bill was before him.

"Stop right where you are!" Bill cried, covering him with his revolver. "Yer'll not git erway this time."

"*Por Dios, señor!*" Manuel replied, piteously, "I must go in and see my wife!"

"That's jest th' ticket," said Bill, "an' I'm th' man what's er goin' ter take yer in ter see her. Come erlong."

Together we entered the open doorway, and the modest patio within. Then, as Manuel stopped at a door, he drew himself up with imposing dignity:

"This is my wife's room, señores," he said, "and I alone must enter."

To my surprise Bill released his arm, and he opened the door. Opposite the door, beside the window, stood the bed, and in it lay Josefa, seemingly asleep, her beauty only intensified by her pallor and the dark circles about her eyes. A groan escaped Manuel's lips, at which her eyes opened wide.

"*A Dios, Manuelito!*" she cried, with a little shriek, "I knew you would come back. You have already forgiven me, I know," she went on, as Manuel threw himself on his knees beside the bed. "*Probecito!* and hast thou also suffered? *Te amo, Manuelito mio!* Why, I have never known before what it is to love! Promise me that you will never leave me again, and I will be a good wife and never torment you any more."

What Manuel may have replied we never knew, for Bill, with a savage grasp on my arm, dragged me away from the door and out into the plaza.

The announcement in the Espiritu Santo of Bill's second failure was greeted with roars of laughter and many jeering remarks. Throughout it all Bill retained his good humor, and ordered drinks for the crowd.

"It's er good un on me," he admitted, cheerfully; "but ef you fellers had er seen her kittenin' up to 'im, you'd say he done right ter knife her. In fact, he'd orter done it soon as old Padre Geronimo got 'em spliced."